L2

E

Please renew/return this item by th
shown. Please call the number below.

Renewals and enquiries: 0300 123 4049

Textphone for hearing or 0300 123 4041
speech impaired users:

www.hertsdirect.org/librarycatalogue

Pearson Education Limited
Edinburgh Gate, Harlow,
Essex CM20 2JE, England
and Associated Companies throughout the world.

ISBN: 978-1-4058-8162-3

Penguin Books edition first published 2003
This edition first published 2008

3 5 7 9 10 8 6 4

Original copyright © 2003
Johnny English is a trademark and copyright of Universal Studios
Licensed by Universal Studios Licensing LLLP. All rights reserved

The moral right of the author has been asserted

Typeset by Graphicraft Ltd, Hong Kong
Set in 11/14pt Bembo
Printed in China
SWTC/03

Published by Pearson Education Ltd in association with
Penguin Books Ltd, both companies being subsidiaries of Pearson Plc

For a complete list of the titles available in the Penguin Readers series please write to your local
Pearson Longman office or to: Penguin Readers Marketing Department, Pearson Education,
Edinburgh Gate, Harlow, Essex CM20 2JE, England.

Contents

Introduction

The Prime Minister wasn't happy.

'Pegasus, we have to do something quickly,' he said. 'Agent One is dead, so who can finish his work?'

'Our best men died at the church,' said Pegasus.

'All of them?' the Prime Minister asked.

'Nearly all of them,' said Pegasus. 'There is one man . . . Johnny English.'

'We'll give him the job,' said the Prime Minister. 'But why wasn't he at the church with the other agents?'

'He was in the car park,' said Pegasus. 'His job that day was . . . security.'

Secret Service agent Johnny English makes mistakes. He often gets the wrong man or is in the wrong place. Now, suddenly, he's England's Number One Agent (but only because of one of his mistakes!). And his first job? Security for the Queen's crown at a party at the Tower of London.

Most of Britain's important people are going to be at the party. Pascal Sauvage is going to be there too. The Frenchman has a plan. First, he wants the Queen's crown. Then he wants to be King of England!

Johnny's job is not going to be easy. Can he do it?

In the film *Johnny English*, Rowan Atkinson is 'England's Number One Agent' and John Malkovich is Pascal Sauvage. Rowan Atkinson is also famous for the very funny Mr Bean films for television and cinema. You can read some of these stories in other Penguin Readers books.

Brittany, France. The house stood high above the sea. *CRACK!* A window broke. A man climbed into the house. Quickly and quietly he began to walk across the dark room.

The light came on.

'VERY GOOD, AGENT ONE!'

Secret Service Agent Number One stopped. He could hear the man – a Frenchman? – but he couldn't see him.

'BUT THIS IS THE END OF YOU! GOODBYE!'

'No!' cried Agent One.

Chapter 1   'Our job is their security.'

Outside a church in England, six men talked.

'A sad day, Agent Five,' said Agent Two.

'Yes,' said Agent Five. 'Agent One was England's greatest Secret Service agent. And now he's dead.'

In the car park, another Secret Service agent watched the cars come in and showed the drivers the way to the church. The agent's name was Bough. He stopped some cars and looked at the drivers' papers.

A long black car arrived with a coffin inside it. Bough put up his hand but a man behind him laughed. The man was Secret Service Agent Johnny English.

'We don't have to stop *this* car, Bough!' said English.

Klein, the driver of the black car, drove past the two agents. Then Vendetta, the man next to him, opened the coffin. He pushed a button.

Minutes later, the six Secret Service agents took the coffin from the car and carried it to the church.

Behind them, the black car drove away – fast!

'There are some very important people in that church, Bough.'

In the car park, English said, 'There are some very important people in that church, Bough. Our job is their security.'

A car stopped next to him. A man looked out of the window. His name was Pegasus and he was the Head of the Secret Service.

'Is everything all right, English?' he asked.

'Yes, sir,' English answered. 'Everything is . . .'

Suddenly, there was a very loud noise from the church behind him and smoke flew up into the sky.

English's face went white. '. . . fine,' he finished weakly.

♦

The Prime Minister wasn't happy.

'Pegasus, we have to do something quickly,' he said. 'Agent One is dead, so who can finish his work?'

'Our best men died at the church,' said Pegasus.

2

'All of them?' the Prime Minister asked.

'Nearly all of them,' said Pegasus. 'There is one man . . . Johnny English.'

'We'll give him the job,' said the Prime Minister. 'But why wasn't he at the church with the other agents?'

'He was in the car park,' said Pegasus. 'His job that day was . . . security.'

'*Security?*' shouted the Prime Minister.

'He sometimes makes mistakes,' said Pegasus unhappily.

Two hours later, English was in Pegasus's office.

'What's this, English?' Pegasus said.

He pushed a button and a television came up from his desk. On the screen was a picture of the Queen's crown.

'It's a . . . nice crown, sir,' said English.

'It's the *Queen's* crown,' Pegasus told him.

Now there was a different picture on the screen. A picture of the Queen with Britain's most important churchman – the Archbishop. It was Queen Elizabeth II's coronation.

'This year, one of Pascal Sauvage's companies cleaned the crown,' said Pegasus. 'And tonight there's a party at the Tower of London. The Queen is going to see the crown there.'

'Pascal Sauvage?' said English. 'That stupid Frenchman? The man with the prison?'

'Sauvage has four hundred prisons in sixty countries,' Pegasus told him. 'He's a friend of the Prime Minister. I want you at the Tower tonight. And no more mistakes.'

Chapter 2   'Let's look at the beautiful crown.'

English and Bough arrived at the Tower of London. Most of Britain's important people were there. At the end of one room was a large box. Inside it was the Queen's crown.

3

A man came across the room to English and Bough.

'I'm Chevenix,' he said. 'Head of Security for the Queen.'

'Are there gunmen on top of the building?' asked English.

'Thirteen of them,' said Chevenix.

'Good,' said English. He saw a very beautiful girl across the room. 'I'm going to talk to people, Chevenix,' he said. He turned to Bough. 'Go and look at the gunmen, Bough.'

◆

Two streets away, a car drove into a garage. It stopped above a hole in the ground. Inside the car, a man opened a door in the floor. He climbed down into the hole and began to walk.

◆

English smiled at the beautiful girl.

'Hello,' he said. 'I'm Johnny English. Who are you? Why are you here?'

'Lorna Campbell,' she said. 'I helped clean the crown. What do you do?'

'Sorry – I can't tell you.' English smiled again.

A tall man with dark eyes came into the room. English didn't see him. His eyes were on Lorna.

The man with the dark eyes walked across the room to English.

'Thank you, waiter,' English said. He took the man's drink.

'Have you met Mr Sauvage?' Lorna asked English.

'No.' English laughed. 'And I don't want to.' He turned to the man again. 'Yes? Can I help you?'

'I'm Pascal Sauvage,' said the man.

'I'm Lorna Campbell,' said Lorna.

English quickly gave Sauvage's drink back to him. 'I'm . . .'

'Johnny English,' Sauvage said. 'I know all about you.'

◆

He saw a very beautiful girl across the room.

Below the room with the crown, Klein took a knife from his coat. Then he walked to a box on the wall.

'And now the lights,' he said.

♦

Sauvage spoke to everybody in the room.

'I want to say. . .' he began.

Suddenly, the lights went out and the room was dark. Security doors closed round the box with the crown in it.

English heard the sound of feet outside the window. A minute later, somebody ran in front of him. English took a bottle from a waiter and hit the person on the head.

The lights came on again.

Everybody looked at the man on the floor.

'That's Chevenix,' said Bough. 'Who hit him?'

English quickly put the bottle behind his back.

'The . . . the man,' he said.

'Man? What man?' asked Sauvage.

'He ran into the next room!' English said. He went into the next room and quickly shut the door. There was nobody there. 'Don't come in!' he shouted to the people in the other room. 'He's got a gun!'

English began to throw chairs across the room.

Outside, Bough and the other people listened to the noise. Then everything went quiet and the door opened. English came out.

'It's all right now,' he said. He quickly shut the door behind him. 'Let's look at the beautiful crown.'

He walked across to the box and pushed a button. The security doors round the box opened.

There was nothing inside it!

Then the Queen arrived.

Chapter 3 'There you are . . . Gunther.'

'I said no mistakes, English,' Pegasus said. It was the next day and they were in Pegasus's office. 'A man hit Chevenix,' said Pegasus. 'You shut him in a room, but what happened to him?'

'He ran away when we were with the Queen,' said English. 'She was . . . suddenly quite ill.'

'We lost her crown!' said Pegasus. 'But we have to find that man. Was he big?'

'Yes,' said English. 'Very . . . big.'

'What colour was his hair?'

'Er . . .' English saw some fruit on a table by the window. 'Orange,' he said.

◆

Pascal Sauvage sat behind his desk in his office. Vendetta stood opposite him. Sauvage laughed.

'English people are stupid, Vendetta,' he said. 'They have bad teeth and their women are ugly. They love that crown, but there was no security. It was easy for me!'

◆

English and Bough were at the Tower.

'Miss Campbell didn't clean the crown,' said Bough. 'The company don't know her.'

'Ah!' said English. 'I knew it!'

Security men and policemen were inside the Tower. There was no crown, but there was a hole in the floor near the box. A big hole.

'How did somebody get in and take the crown?' English said.

Bough's eyes were on the hole in the floor.

'Sir!' he said. 'There's a h—'

'Quiet, Bough!' English told him. 'I'm thinking.' He moved

7

nearer the hole. 'Did he come through the window?' He was *very* near the hole now. 'Or the floor?' He gave a little laugh. 'No, not the fl—'

English began to fall back into the hole.

Bough caught him, then the two of them looked down. It was very dark.

'One of us has to go down, Bough,' English said.

Minutes later, Bough was halfway down the hole.

'It's not very wide now,' he called up. 'I can't move.'

'Wait there!' said English angrily. 'I'm coming down.'

He climbed into the hole – and fell on to Bough. The two of them fell to the bottom.

'I'm sitting on something,' said English. 'What is it?'

'Me, sir,' Bough answered.

They stood up.

'Look!' Bough said.

They could see light . . . and a hand. The hand pulled a bag up through another hole.

English and Bough ran to the other hole and looked out.

He climbed into the hole.

8

They could see a garage. Outside the garage, there was a long black car. Vendetta and Klein put the crown into a coffin. On the coffin was the word 'Mum' in flowers.

English climbed up out of the hole and Bough followed him. Vendetta and Klein turned. Vendetta had a gun, but English quickly shot it out of his hand.

Klein took something from his coat and threw it. Suddenly, there was smoke everywhere. Then English and Bough heard the long black car drive away. They ran outside.

A small red car stopped behind them. Lorna Campbell was inside it. She saw the black car and drove after it.

English ran through the streets to the Tower of London. Bough ran after him, but English was too fast. He jumped into his car and drove after the black car.

'Wait!' shouted Bough, from the road.

English didn't hear him. After a minute, he turned round.

'Bough?' he said. 'Where are you? Oh . . .'

Three hundred metres away, he could see a long black car.

'That's it!' said English, and he drove after it.

The car stopped outside a church. English watched the coffin come out. On the coffin was the word 'Dad' in flowers.

English took a small radio from his coat and spoke into it.

'Bough, I'm at Brompton church,' he said. 'They're putting the coffin into the ground.'

'Wait for me, sir!' Bough said.

Some minutes later, Bough got out of a taxi near the church. He saw a long black car go past, fast. On the coffin inside, flowers made the word 'Mum'.

A small red car with Lorna Campbell inside went after it.

♦

The coffin was in a hole in the ground. People stood round the hole. Some of them cried.

English walked to them with his gun in his hand. He jumped down into the hole, on top of the coffin.

Some of the people began to shout 'Stop!' and 'What are you doing?' and 'Get out of there!'

English laughed. 'Are you going to come here again later and take it out of the ground?' He put his gun near the head of a man in a black hat. 'Who are you?'

'I'm the driver,' the man said.

English smiled. 'You're the . . .' He stopped. This wasn't Klein. Or Vendetta. Something was wrong. The crown wasn't in this coffin. There was a *dead person* in this coffin.

Then Bough arrived. Everybody looked at him.

'Ah,' said Bough. 'There you are . . . Gunther.'

'G–Gunther?' said English.

'Yes, Gunther!' said Bough. He looked at the people round the coffin. 'I'm . . . Doctor Bough. He's not . . . very well.' He looked down at English. 'Give me the gun, Gunther. Good boy. That's right. Now let's get you out of there.'

English climbed up out of the hole. He took Bough's hand and walked away with him.

Chapter 4   'Don't go near Pascal Sauvage!'

Inside his office, Sauvage opened the coffin. He smiled. Then he took out the crown and put it above his head.

'We have to have an archbishop,' said Vendetta.

'We'll have an archbishop,' Sauvage told him.

'And Johnny English?'

Sauvage took a video from his desk and played a short film on his screen. The film showed English at his home in his bathroom. The agent's hands were up in front of his face, and he made a gun with his fingers.

He made a gun with his fingers.

'You see?' said Sauvage. 'English is stupid. He plays games. When you see him again, kill him.'

♦

Bough showed Pegasus pictures of Klein and Vendetta.

'They came out of prison last year,' he said.

'They work for one of Sauvage's companies,' said English.

'What are you saying?' said Pegasus. 'Pascal Sauvage took the crown? Never! He's a great man. Forget Sauvage and go back to work. I'm going to a party tonight. Find me when you really know something. And don't go near Pascal Sauvage!'

English and Bough went down to the car park.

'I want an aeroplane, Bough,' said English. 'I want it ready for tonight. And two parachutes.' He saw a man under one of the cars. 'Good afternoon, Felch.'

The man under the car didn't answer.

'Why do we want an aeroplane?' asked Bough.

'Because tonight we're going to go into Sauvage's offices,' said English.

'But Pegasus said—' began Bough.

'I know, but . . .' English stopped. 'Wait! *Was* that Felch under the car?'

They turned and saw Vendetta! He had a gun and began to shoot. English and Bough jumped out of the way. Vendetta ran and Bough shot at him. English pulled out his gun. It broke and fell to the floor.

Bough moved behind a car and took a radio from his coat. He spoke into it.

'Can you see him, sir?' he asked English.

English looked under a car and saw two legs.

'Yes, I can see him,' he answered quietly. The legs moved and English followed them. 'I'm getting him . . . *now!*' He jumped on to the man and pushed him to the floor. '*Got you!*'

They turned and saw Vendetta!

Then he looked down and saw Bough on the floor below him. Bough didn't move.

English turned and saw Vendetta run out of the car park.

♦

'*Somebody* pulled me down, sir,' said Bough. 'And it wasn't Vendetta. Were there two of them?'

He and English were inside the aeroplane. They wore parachutes. Below them was the city of London.

'Er... yes, that's right, Bough,' said English.

Bough turned on his computer and showed English a picture of two tall buildings.

'We want this building, here. I jump first, on to *here*. Then I climb down to this window...'

'I know all this!' said English. He wasn't very interested. 'I jump on to *here* and climb down to that window.'

A red light came on in front of them.

'It's nearly time, sir,' said Bough.

He opened the door of the aeroplane.

The green JUMP light came on and Bough jumped out into the night sky. He used the wind and flew down to the top of Sauvage's building. He quickly took off his parachute and climbed down to the right window.

English jumped out of the aeroplane. Down he went, on to the top of a tall building. He took off his parachute and climbed down to a window. He broke it and climbed inside. Then he took out his radio.

'Where now, Bough?' he said into it.

'Go out of the room and across the next room to the door on your right,' Bough told him. 'That's Sauvage's office.'

English left the room and found the other door. He opened it and went inside. Everything was dark. He turned on the light and saw an old man in a hospital bed.

'A prisoner!' he said. 'What did he do to you?'

'My teeth—' began the old man. He couldn't talk because his mouth hurt.

'He took out some of your *teeth*?' said English. 'What are they *doing* in this place? I have to get you out of here!'

He pulled the old man out of the bed and through a door into the next room. There he found more people in hospital beds.

A man in a white coat came into the room. English quickly took out his gun.

'Are you Sauvage's doctor?' he asked.

'I'm a doctor,' the man said. 'What's happening?'

'What are you doing?' asked English. 'Selling teeth? Cutting off arms and legs and selling them too?'

'What are you talking about?' said the doctor.

English turned and looked out of the window. Across the road he could see a big building – the biggest building in London. In lights was the word SAUVAGE. Bough's face looked out of one of the windows.

14

'*I'm in the wrong building,*' English thought. 'Er . . .' He gave a little laugh. 'I'm Johnny English, Secret Service agent,' he said. 'I'm . . . looking at your security. And it's . . . OK! Everything's OK. So I'll go now.'

Chapter 5   'I'm going to be King of England!'

English and Bough moved through the Sauvage building.

'You came down on the wrong building,' said Bough.

'No, Bough. I . . . I wanted to look at the other building,' said English. 'I—'

'Somebody's coming!' Bough said.

They quickly moved into a dark place and waited. A minute later, Sauvage and a woman went past them.

Then English said, 'All right, Bough, we can go—'

'Wait!' somebody said.

English looked behind him and saw a security man with a gun. English moved quickly. He had two pens in his coat – one red, one black. He pushed the red pen into the security man's arm. At the same time, Bough hit the man on the head. He fell to the floor.

'Good work, Bough,' said English. He showed Bough the red pen. 'But you didn't have to do that. One push with this pen and people can't walk or talk.'

He turned and looked through an open door. He could see two men. One man put a mask on to the other man's face.

'It's the Archbishop's face!' said Bough. 'But it isn't the Archbishop!'

After the two men left through another door, English and Bough went into the room. Through a third door, at the back, they could see Sauvage's office.

'Let's go,' said English.

Bough started to look through the things on Sauvage's desk.

English found a video and looked for a television. But he put his hand on a button by accident and a second video began to play on a screen behind him. There were pictures of London and of Westminster Abbey. Then Sauvage came on to the screen and talked to the camera.

'England, wonderful England!' he said. 'Or is it? English hospitals are dirty. Trains are late and there are a lot of cars on the roads. So why do I want to live there? What do I want from this country? What does England have? Answer: it has a QUEEN! And a queen can do *everything*. She can *have* everything! When she speaks, people listen. So what will *I* do when I'm King of England? Because I'm *going* to be King of England!'

Suddenly, Klein came into the room.

English pulled out his gun.

'Don't move, Klein,' he said.

'I'm not going to tell you anything, English,' said Klein.

'Yes, you are.' English took a black pen from his coat. 'This will help.' He pushed the pen into Klein's arm. 'Now, why does Sauvage want to be king?'

'I'm not g-g-gloooing fl-l-l . . .' said Klein, and fell.

Bough caught him.

'Perhaps you use the *red* pen when you want people to talk,' he said to English. 'And the *black* pen . . .'

'Don't be stupid, Bough,' said English. He pushed the black pen into his hand. 'This makes you . . . t-l-l-a-w-f-f-l-l . . .'

He fell down on the floor.

A security man came into the office. He looked at English and took out his gun. Then a chair hit him across the back of the head and he fell. The person with the chair was Lorna.

'Let's get out of here,' she said to Bough.

Bough and Lorna half-carried English through the building and down the stairs.

'Who *are* you?' Bough asked her.

16

'I'm going to be King of England!'

'Lorna Campbell, from Interpol,'* she said. 'We know Sauvage. Every important prisoner from a Sauvage prison works for him after they come out. He's going to do something big and very bad. What will it be? We don't know.'

'Want to see Plegashushhhh,' said English.

◆

Downstairs in the same building, Pascal Sauvage was at a party with the most important people in London.

English, Bough and Lorna came into the room.

'I'm going to find Pegasus,' Bough told Lorna.

Lorna saw Klein move slowly across the floor to Sauvage.

A waiter went past and English took a drink from him. He turned round. The glass fell out of his hand and down the front of a woman's dress.

'Sl-l-lorry!' he said.

'Let's dance,' Lorna said quickly.

Across the room, Klein talked to Sauvage. Sauvage listened angrily.

Bough found Pegasus.

'Sir,' he said. 'I have—'

Sauvage suddenly stopped next to them.

'Pegasus,' he said, 'this man and his boss, English, went into my office this evening. And they hurt three of my security men.'

English and Lorna danced past them.

'Outside, English!' Pegasus shouted. 'Bough, go home.'

◆

'What did I tell you? Forget Sauvage!' said Pegasus. 'So what do you do? You go into his office and hit his security men on the head!'

'Sir,' said English. 'Perrlaaaps I c-can—'

* Interpol: Policemen and policewomen from different countries work for Interpol

'Go home,' said Pegasus. 'Forget this job. I never want to hear your name again. Do you understand?'

♦

In a very large house in the country, the Queen walked into her office. Five men waited for her. One of them was Vendetta. He had a gun.

He put a paper on her desk.

'This letter says, "I am going to abdicate, and nobody in my family will be queen or king." ' he told her. 'Now write your name at the bottom.'

The Queen looked at the gun but didn't move.

Vendetta had one of the Queen's dogs. He put his gun to the dog's head.

'Do it!' he said.

The Queen wrote her name.

♦

The next day, a man with the Archbishop's mask on his face came out of the Prime Minister's house. He got into a car.

'All OK?' asked the driver.

'Easy!' said the man in the mask.

Two hours later, Pascal Sauvage arrived at the same house. The Prime Minister was in his office.

'The Queen is abdicating,' he told Sauvage. He showed Sauvage the letter. 'She's tired after fifty years and her children don't want the job. So . . . you are our next king.'

'Me?' said Sauvage. 'King?'

'Yes,' the Prime Minister answered. 'You're from the same family. Look! I've got all the papers here. After Queen Elizabeth and her family abdicate, you're the next king. I know that you're a very busy man. But you love this country – and England wants you. Will you do the job?'

'Me?' said Sauvage. 'King?'

Sauvage smiled at the Prime Minister.
'OK!' he said.

♦

English walked out of his flat and saw Lorna.
'Sauvage is going to his house in Brittany,' she said. 'He's going to have a party for some rich people. We're going too.'
'Sorry,' said English. 'I'm not working for Pegasus—'
'No, you're working for me,' she told him.

Chapter 6   'The King! The King!'

They sat in a café in Brittany. They could see Sauvage's house, high above the sea. Lorna drank some of her coffee.

'Why did Sauvage have to take the crown?' she asked. 'It will be his crown when he's king.'

'He wanted the Queen to abdicate,' said English. 'He had plans – but sometimes things go wrong. With the crown, he could be "king" to his French friends. He could have a "coronation". But now, when that crown comes down on his head, Sauvage will really be king. What will he do to our country? I love England! We have to stop him!'

Lorna looked at him with love in her eyes.

An hour later, she and English were inside Sauvage's house.

'Which way?' he asked her.

'This door,' she said. 'I can hear people.'

She opened the door slowly. They were high above a big room. Below them, ten men sat round a table. They watched a large screen. It showed Pascal Sauvage's face.

'. . . and I am going to be the new King of England,' Sauvage said. 'And why do I want to be king of that stupid little country? I'll tell you. What does every country have? Killers and other prisoners. A lot of them. "We don't want them in our country," people say. "What can we do with them?" I have the answer to that question, and it will make us rich. We will take prisoners from every country in the world – *and we will put them in England!* When I'm king, I'm going to make England the biggest prison in the world! So, who wants to buy some of my little country?'

Up above them, English said quietly, 'We have to get that video! We have to show it to Pegasus.' He put his hand on the wall – and, by accident, pushed a button. Suddenly, everybody in the room could hear his words: 'THEY DON'T KNOW THAT WE'RE HERE, LORNA. I'M GOING TO JUMP DOWN. THEN YOU CAN COME IN THROUGH THE DOOR AND WE WILL MAKE SAUVAGE OUR PRISONER. OK? GO!'

The men at the table looked at Sauvage.

He smiled and waited.

English jumped down, next to the video player. He took out his gun.

'Stand up!' he told Sauvage.

English took the video out of the player but it fell from his hand. He didn't look down, but he found it. Then he put it in his coat.

'Look behind you, Mr English,' Sauvage said.

English laughed. 'Why?' he said. 'Are there four men with guns behind me? I don't think there are, Sauvage.'

'I do,' Sauvage answered.

English turned. There *were* four men with guns behind him. Lorna was there too. She was Klein's prisoner.

The security men took English's gun.

'Take them away,' said Sauvage.

They took English and Lorna to a small dark room.

'We have to get out,' English said. 'Sauvage's coronation is in seven hours. How can we get that door open?'

And then somebody kicked the door open.

It was Bough.

♦

The world's most important people were in Westminster Abbey. The Prime Minister was there, and Pegasus. Outside, thousands of people were in the streets of London for the coronation of King Pascal. The world watched on television.

Sauvage walked to the front of the Abbey. Television cameras followed him. The Archbishop was there with the crown.

Sauvage sat down in the large coronation chair.

Suddenly, English ran through the Abbey.

'Stop!' he shouted. 'You can't make this man King of England!'

Security men ran to English, but Sauvage stopped them.

'We have to get out,' English said.

'Let's hear him,' he said.

Above them, at the top of some stairs, Vendetta looked down. He had a gun.

English spoke to the television cameras. The people in the Abbey could see his face on a big screen.

'This man Sauvage is a killer. And that man in front of him is not the Archbishop. His face is a mask!'

English put his hands on the Archbishop's face and pulled. And pulled . . . Nothing happened.

Vendetta got his gun ready. Suddenly, a foot pushed him to the floor. He looked up and saw Lorna.

Below them, English pulled the Archbishop's hair. It stayed on the man's head.

'OK,' said English. 'I was wrong about that. But . . . Bough, play the video!'

Bough was with the television people, high up in the Abbey. He put a video into a video player. The picture came up on screens in the Abbey and on televisions round the world. It was a film – of Johnny English in his bathroom. He made a gun with his fingers.

Vendetta tried to shoot Lorna, but she pulled the gun out of his hand. Then she hit him with it and he didn't move again.

Sauvage said to the Archbishop, 'Finish the coronation!'

The Archbishop spoke the words slowly and carefully. Then he took the crown and put it above Sauvage's head.

'*This is it!*' thought Sauvage. '*When that crown comes down on my head, I will be King of England!*'

English jumped up behind him and took the crown. Then he ran to some stairs.

Sauvage took out his gun and shouted, 'Give that crown to me!'

He shot at English. The crown fell from English's hand and down the stairs. It stopped at the Archbishop's feet. English ran after it.

24

Sauvage turned to the Archbishop.

'Do it!' he shouted.

The Archbishop took the crown and started to put it down on to Sauvage's head.

'And now you are . . .'

English pushed Sauvage. The crown came down . . . on to English's head!

'. . . king!' finished the Archbishop.

And everybody started to shout, 'The King! The King!'

Slowly, English began to smile. Sauvage began to cry.

♦

Three days later, English and Lorna sat in English's car above a beach in the south of France.

'What did the Queen say?' Lorna asked him.

'She said, "Thank you for everything." I think she loves me,' said English. He laughed.

'I love you too,' Lorna said.

English put his arm round her. And, by accident, he put his hand on a button.

The top of the car opened – and Lorna went up into the sky! She came down in the sea.

She smiled. 'Oh, Johnny!' she said.

ACTIVITIES

Chapters 1–2

Before you read

1   What stories about Secret Service agents do you know?
2   Look at the Word List at the back of the book.
    a   Which are words:
        for people?   for buildings?
    b   Which words can you use when you talk about kings and
        queens?
3   Read the Introduction to the book and answer the questions.
    a   What happened in a church?
    b   What is Johnny English's first important job?
    c   What is Pascal Sauvage's plan?

While you read

4   Finish the sentences with one of these names:
    Agent One   Agent Five   Bough   Johnny English   Klein
    Lorna Campbell   Pascal Sauvage   Pegasus
    a   .... dies in France.
    b   .... tries to stop the black car with the coffin.
    c   .... is the Head of the Secret Service.
    d   .... dies in the church.
    e   .... is a friend of the Prime Minister and has four
        hundred prisons.
    f   .... helped clean the Queen's crown.
    g   .... cuts the lights in the Tower of London.
    h   .... hits the wrong man.

After you read

5   Why does Johnny English
    a   not want Bough to stop the black car?
    b   not die in the church?
    c   get an important job?
    d   send Bough to the top of a building?
    e   not see Pascal Sauvage when he comes in?

    f take Pascal Sauvage's drink?

    g hit Chevenix with a bottle?

    h throw chairs across a room?

6 Work with another student. Have this conversation between Johnny English and Lorna Campbell.

    Student A: You are Lorna Campbell. You want to know about English's job. Ask questions. Can you get any answers?

    Student B: You are Johnny English. You like Lorna. Answer her questions, but don't tell her about your job.

Chapter 3

Before you read

7 Discuss these questions.

    a What will happen when Pegasus talks to Johnny English? Why?

    b Look at the picture on page 8. What is Johnny English doing? What is he going to do? Why?

While you read

8 Are these sentences right (✓) or wrong (✗)?

    a English tells Pegasus that he hit Chevenix.   .....

    b English saw a man with orange hair.   .....

    c Vendetta and Klein work for Pascal Sauvage.   .....

    d Bough and English see Vendetta and Klein outside a garage.   .....

    e Lorna Campbell drives after Klein and Vendetta.   .....

    f English follows Klein and Vendetta to a church.   .....

    g The people at the church think that Bough is a doctor.   .....

After you read

9 Who is speaking? Who to? Why?

    a 'Orange.'

    b 'The company don't know her.'

    c 'There's a h—'

    d 'They're putting the coffin into the ground.'

    e 'Get out of there!'

f 'Are you going to come here again later and take it out of the ground?'

g 'There you are . . . Gunther.'

10 Work with another student. Have this conversation between Pegasus and Johnny English.

Student A: You are Pegasus. You are angry with Johnny English. You want him to lose his job. Tell him why.

Student B: You are Johnny English. You think that you are a good Secret Service agent. Tell Pegasus why.

11 Answer these questions with other students.

a What does Pascal Sauvage think about English people? Why?

b Why does Johnny English go to the church?

c How does Johnny English know that he is standing on the wrong coffin?

d How does Bough help English in this chapter?

Chapter 4

Before you read

12 In this chapter, Johnny English wants an aeroplane and two parachutes. What is his plan, do you think?

While you read

13 What happens first? And then? Number the sentences 1–8.

a English pulls a man out of bed.   .....

b English and Bough talk to Pegasus about Pascal Sauvage.   .....

c English talks to a doctor.   .....

d Vendetta tries to kill English.   .....

e English knows that he is in the wrong building.   .....

f English jumps on the wrong man.   .....

g English and Bough jump out of an aeroplane.   .....

h Sauvage and Vendetta see a video of Johnny English.   .....

After you read

14 Who and what are these sentences about?

a He wants an archbishop.

b There is a video camera in his bathroom.

   c He thinks that English and Bough are wrong.

   d He doesn't say 'Good afternoon'.

   e He doesn't shoot his gun in the car park.

   f He thinks that Vendetta had a friend in the car park.

   g He doesn't listen carefully.

   h English thinks that they are Sauvage's prisoners.

15 Discuss these sentences with other students. Do you think they are right? Why (not)?

   a 'Bough is cleverer than English.'

   b 'Pegasus is a bad boss.'

Chapter 5

Before you read

16 Look at the picture on page 17. Why does Pascal Sauvage want to be the King of England? Will he be a good king? Why (not)?

While you read

17 Underline the right answer.

   a English pushes a *black / red* pen into the security man's arm.

   b One of Sauvage's men is wearing a *crown / mask*.

   c English watches a video of *the Queen's coronation / Pascal Sauvage*.

   d English wants Klein to *fall down / talk*.

   e Lorna Campbell works for *Sauvage / the police*.

   f Sauvage invited *Lorna Campbell / Pegasus* to his party.

   g The Queen of England loves *cats / dogs*.

   h *The Archbishop / One of Sauvage's men* visits the Prime Minister.

   i *Lorna Campbell / Pegasus* wants English to go to Brittany.

After you read

18 How do these people feel, and why?

   a Pascal Sauvage, about England

   b English, after he pushes the black pen into Klein's arm

   c Bough, when he meets Lorna Campbell for the first time

   d Sauvage, after Klein talks to him at the party

    e Pegasus, about Johnny English

    f the Queen, after Vendetta visits her

    g Sauvage, after he talks to the Prime Minister

19 Work with another student. Have this conversation between Lorna Campbell and her boss at Interpol.

    Student A: You are Lorna Campbell. You want to take Johnny English to Brittany with you. Tell your boss why.

    Student B: You are Lorna's boss. You don't want English to go to Brittany with Lorna. Tell her why.

Chapter 6

Before you read

20 At the end of the story, will Sauvage be King of England? Why (not)? Discuss these questions with other students.

While you read

21 <u>Underline</u> the wrong word in each sentence. What is the right word?

    a Lorna and English leave the hotel and go to Sauvage's house. ....

    b In the room above Lorna and English, ten men are watching a video of Pascal Sauvage. ....

    c When English accidentally pushes a button, everybody in the room can see him. ....

    d English takes Sauvage's gun and puts it in his coat. ....

    e When English pulls the king's face, Vendetta takes out his gun. ....

    f Bough shows the world a video of Johnny English in a hospital. ....

    g The Archbishop takes the crown and tries to put it on English's head. ....

After you read

22 How do these people feel at the end of the story? Why? Discuss your answers with other students.

    a Johnny English   **d** Pascal Sauvage

    b Lorna Campbell   **e** the Queen of England

    c Pegasus

Writing

23 You are Pegasus. Write about Johnny English at the end of the story. What mistakes did he make? Will he stay in his job? Why (not)?

24 What happens to Pascal Sauvage, Klein and Vendetta at the end of the story? Write about them.

25 You are Bough. Your best friend wants to work for the Secret Service too. Write him a letter and tell him the good and bad things about life in the Secret Service.

26 Write a funny short story about Johnny English and Lorna Campbell on holiday in the south of France. What goes wrong? Does Lorna love Johnny at the end of the holiday? Why (not)?

27 You are Bough. You like Johnny English, but you don't want to work with him again. Write him a letter and tell him your feelings.

28 You are Johnny English after you read Bough's letter (Question 27). You think that Bough is wrong. You don't think that you made any mistakes. You know that you are the best agent in the Secret Service. Write Bough a letter and tell him why.

29 You work for a newspaper. Write about King Pascal's coronation (Chapter 6) for your newspaper.

30 How are these important in the story? Write two or three sentences about each of them.

    a coffins   **b** Lorna Campbell   **c** videos   **d** parties

WORD LIST *with example sentences*

abbey (n) Westminster *Abbey* is a very important church in London.

abdicate (v) Edward VIII *abdicated* in 1936 because he wanted to marry an American woman.

agent (n) James Bond is a British *agent*.

archbishop (n) The *Archbishop* of Canterbury is an important person in the Church of England.

button (n) He pushed a *button* and the door opened.

coffin (n) When they put the *coffin* in the ground, the family cried.

coronation (n) Elizabeth II's *coronation* was in 1953.

crown (n) Elizabeth II doesn't always wear a *crown*!

hole (n) My feet are wet because there are *holes* in my shoes.

king (n) Charles will be *king* after his mother, Elizabeth II, dies.

mask (n) The woman is wearing a *mask*, so you can't see her face.

parachute (n) He jumped from the aeroplane and opened his *parachute*.

prime minister (n) Margaret Thatcher and Tony Blair were British *prime ministers*.

prison (n) He is a very bad man. Send him to *prison*!

queen (n) Elizabeth II is *Queen* of the United Kingdom, but also of Canada, Australia and other countries.

screen (n) There was a large television *screen* on the wall.

secret service (n) James Bond works for the British *Secret Service*.

security (n) My brother works at night. He is a *security* man at a bank.

shoot (v) Put down your gun! Don't *shoot*!

tower (n) You can see a long way from the top of the church *tower*.